Flying Fiddle Duets

for Violin and Viola

Book One   Myanna Harvey

CHP344

©2018 by C. Harvey Publications All Rights Reserved.

www.charveypublications.com

Cover painting by Gregory El Harvey
For more information, visit www.gregharveygallery.com

Flying Fiddle Duets for Violin and Viola

Traditional Tunes, arranged by Myanna Harvey

Table of Contents

Title	Page
1. John Ryan's Polka	2
2. The Irish Washerwoman	4
3. Swallowtail Jig	6
4. Johnny's Gone for a Soldier	7
5. Drunken Sailor	8
6. Greensleeves	10
7. Soldier's Joy	12
8. Star of the County Down	14
9. The Water is Wide	15
10. Lannigan's Ball	16
11. 1812 Quickstep	18
12. Shenandoah	20
13. All the Pretty Horses	22
14. Fire in the Mountain	24
15. Devil Among the Tailors	26
16. Liberty	28
17. The Girl I Left Behind Me	30
18. Ballad of the Green Mountain Boys	32
19. St. Patrick's Day	34

Flying Fiddle Duets for Violin and Viola, Book One

John Ryan's Polka

Trad., arr. Myanna Harvey

©2018 C. Harvey Publications. All Rights Reserved.

The Irish Washerwoman

Trad., arr. M. Harvey

©2018 C. Harvey Publications. All Rights Reserved.

Swallowtail Jig

Trad., arr. M. Harvey

Johnny's Gone for a Soldier

Trad., arr. M. Harvey

Drunken Sailor

Trad., arr. M. Harvey

©2018 C. Harvey Publications. All Rights Reserved.

Greensleeves

Trad., arr. M. Harvey

Soldier's Joy

Trad., arr. M. Harvey

©2018 C. Harvey Publications. All Rights Reserved.

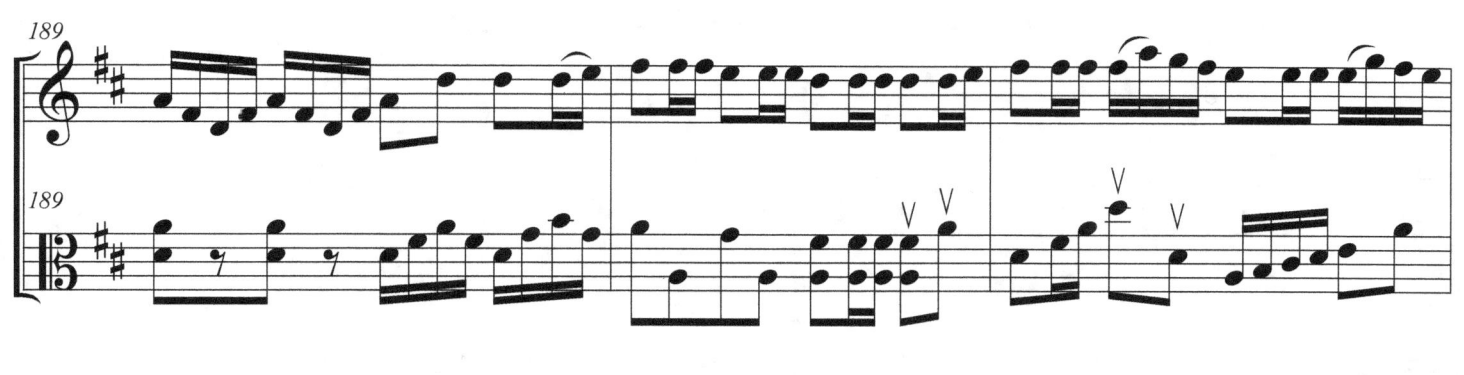
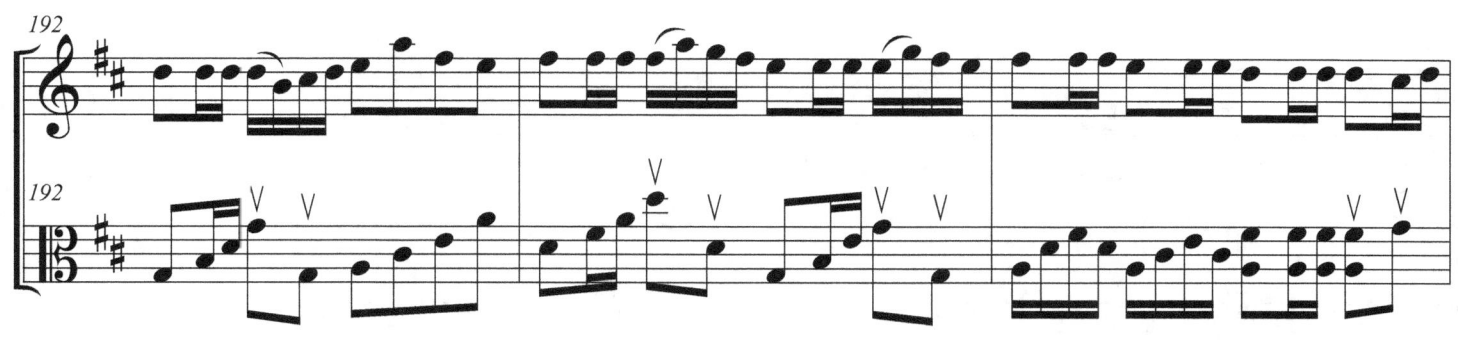
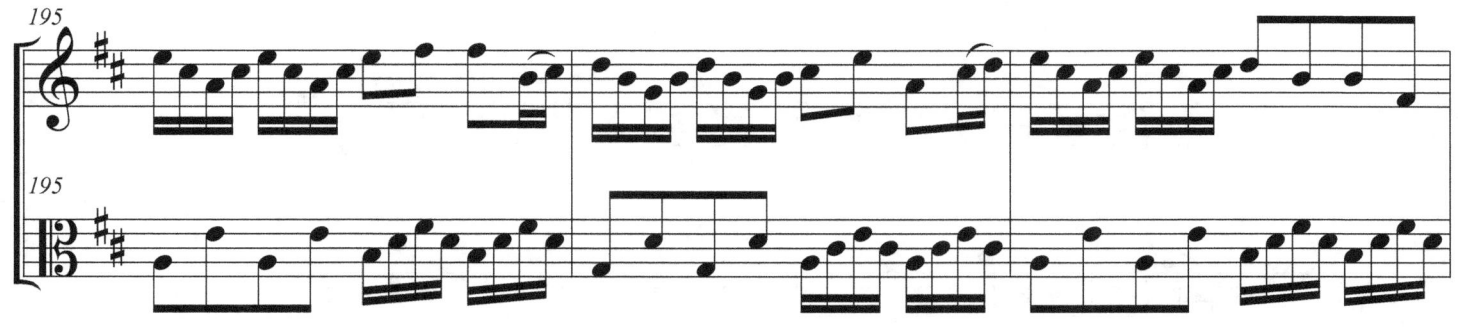
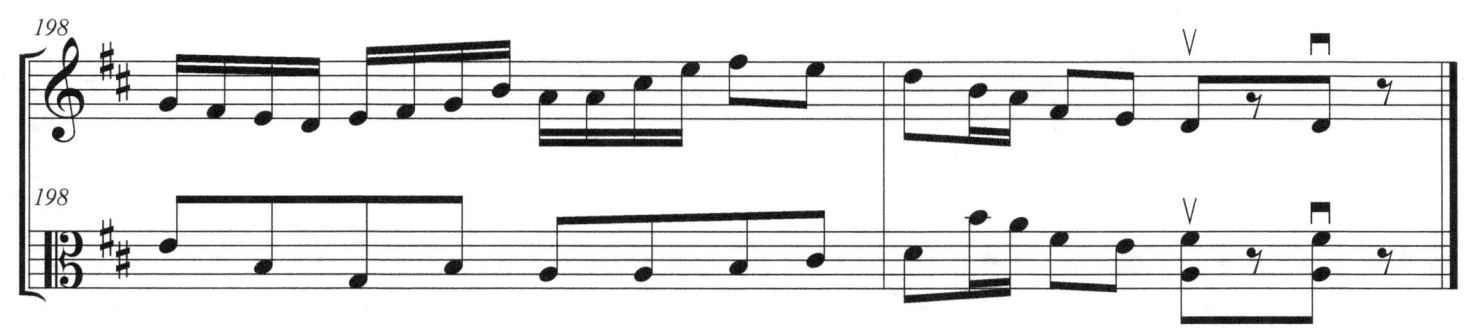

Star of the County Down

Trad., arr. M. Harvey

The Water is Wide

Trad., arr. M. Harvey

Lannigan's Ball

Trad., arr. M. Harvey

©2018 C. Harvey Publications. All Rights Reserved.

Flying Fiddle Duets for Violin and Viola

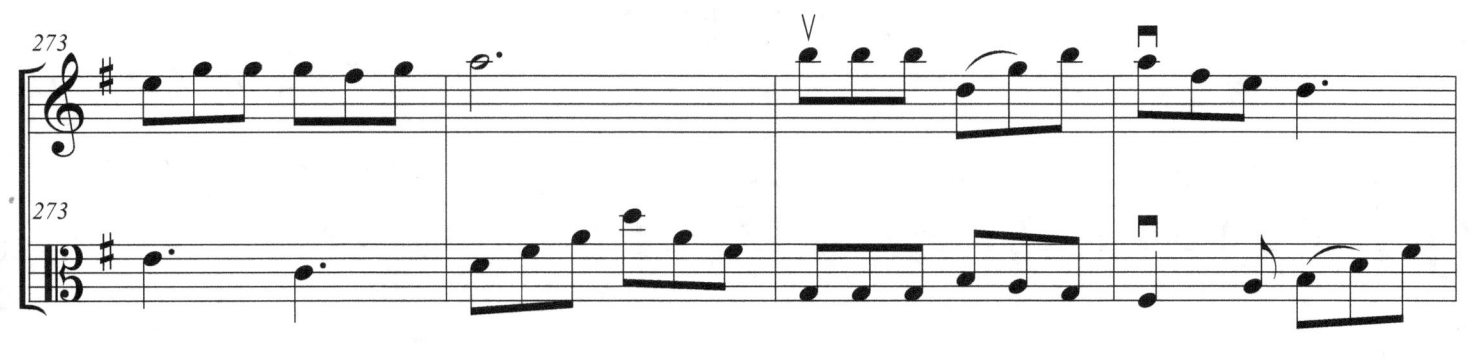

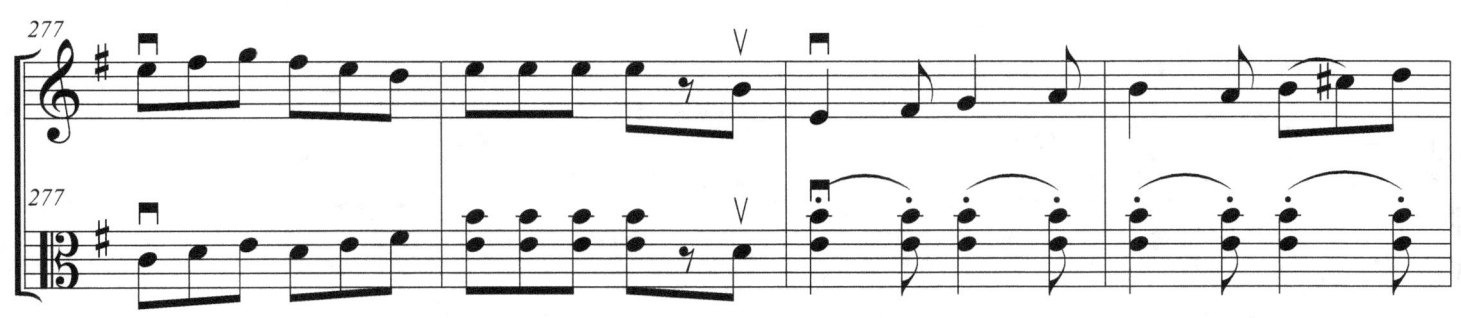

1812 Quickstep

Trad., arr. M. Harvey

©2018 C. Harvey Publications. All Rights Reserved.

Shenandoah

Trad., arr. M. Harvey

©2018 C. Harvey Publications. All Rights Reserved.

All the Pretty Horses

Trad., arr. M. Harvey

**This Page Left Blank
to Eliminate Page Turns**

Fire in the Mountain

Trad., arr. M. Harvey

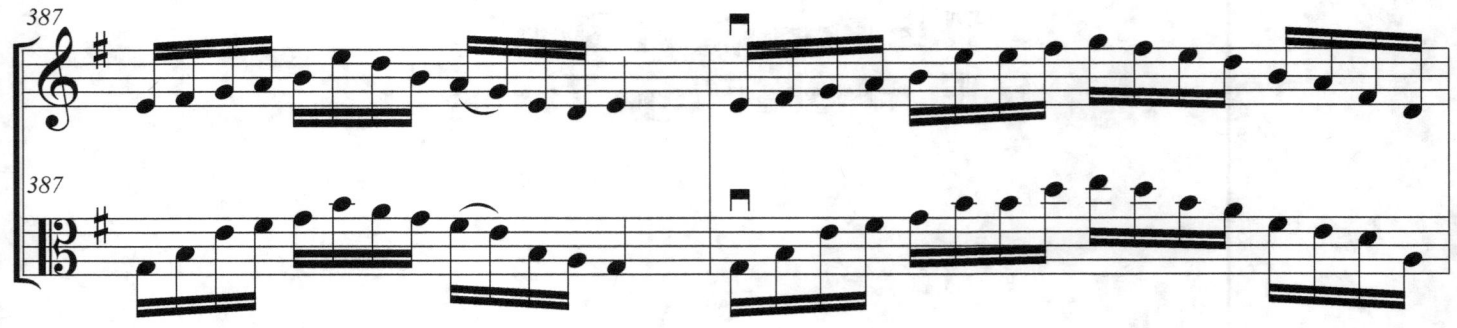

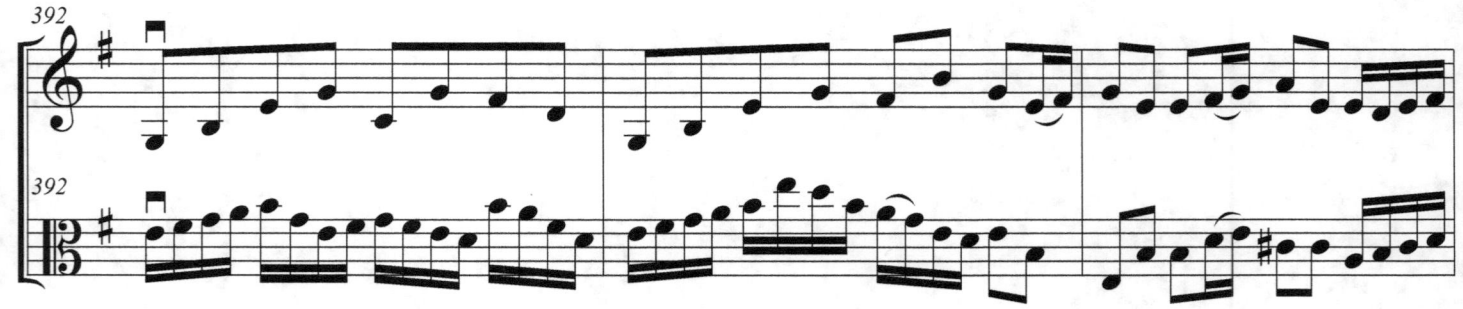

©2018 C. Harvey Publications. All Rights Reserved.

Devil Among the Tailors

Trad., arr. M. Harvey

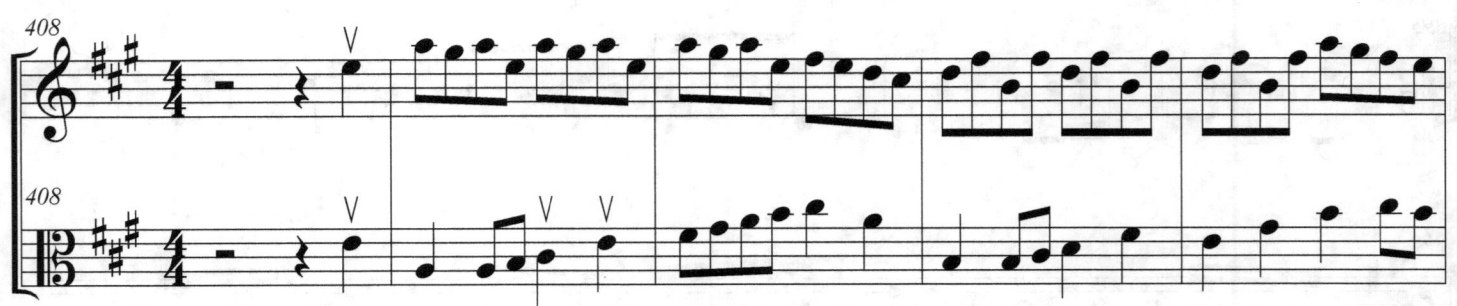

©2018 C. Harvey Publications. All Rights Reserved.

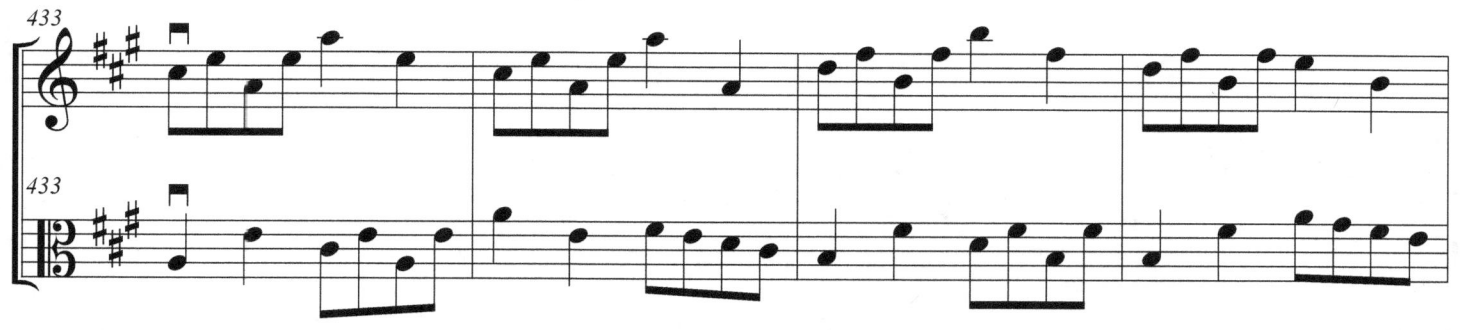

Liberty

Trad., arr. M. Harvey

The Girl I Left Behind Me

Trad., arr. M. Harvey

Ballad of the Green Mountain Boys

Trad., arr. M. Harvey

St. Patrick's Day

Trad., arr. M. Harvey

www.ingramcontent.com/pod-product-compliance
Lightning Source LLC
Chambersburg PA
CBHW051427070526
44584CB00023B/3621